Awakening with Sunrise

Golden rays on empty sand beaches

As if nature revealing our breaches,

A sight so poignant, sad and rare

Calls us to respect, love and care,

Crowning glory of sun spread as liquid red gold

Inspiring us to be hopeful, strong and bold,

These times of test will not stay forever

United we will emerge being stronger,

Each zestful sunrise and elegant sunset

Forward life's journey for promises to be kept.

Tiny Steps make the Way

We are all on a journey called life.

Maybe still far from our dreams but each step in the right direction is taking us closer to realising them and making our manifestations our reality.

Simplicity is Beautiful

The laws of the universe are so simple and uncomplicated.

Some mornings, I just pause and admire the small acts of nature.

Get rid of any complexities whether in interactions

or relations with others.

Life does not have to be hard or complex, try and simplify it.

Resonating Positivity

When we are in a state of gratitude, we are resonating positive thoughts and energy from our inner core out to the universe.

Let this resonance of our positivity grow to create an aura of calmness, peace and stability all around us.

Power of Silent Prayers

When you feel the world is falling around you

A silent prayer of heart will see you through.

Say an extra prayer sincerely for someone

who might be needing it more than you.

Who knows how many hearts are bleeding tonight

With just an extra prayer you might help them see that light.

Every time you help a stranger with an extra prayer or two

You are piling secret blessings that will all reach back to you.

Humility is Divinity

You are awesome when you are humble.

Humility brings a fresher version of you
and spreads pleasantness to everyone around you.

By being humble we are truly closer to being divine.

Stay in the Game

Despite the darkness hold on to your flame

Tumbling or falling still stay in the game

There's hope and trust the plot will change

Unfailingly you will thrive and rise again

Legacy of Positivity

Remain steadfast to your core values of doing good and seeing the good in others. Rather than worrying on returns from others, spend your time in building this legacy of seeing positivity in every life situation.

Resilience

Your body may be battered and bruised

but your spirit is indestructible. Take a deep breath,

dust yourself off and start again. Focus on what you value most,

and you will succeed.

Mantra for Happiness

You always gain by giving

You always rise by sharing

You always grow by caring

You always achieve by daring

Growing through your Pain

Pain affects us all in different ways.

Do not devalue your pain; it too has a purpose in our life.

Make it a source of your strength as you are

going through these experiences.

It is helping us grow strong mentally by enduring these

and developing empathy towards pain of others.

Voyage of Life

The wind charts the course with waves today

Inspiring us to get up and navigate our way

Shape our passions, knot our dreams and set our sails

Journey of life is nothing but sum of success and fails.

Let Trust overcome Fear

When fears gather in the heart like dark clouds in the skies

Transforming gentle emotions to say our final goodbyes

Let the trust in God's love carry you over sorrow

Wiping teary eyes and replacing life in your hollow.

Ask for Help

There might be a struggle along the way

There might be a heartbreak and pain today

It might make no sense, and everything is cloudy

Do not waver, be bold and ask for help today.

Inspiration has no Expiry

Let the waves today wash away all the fears

Hold close your loved ones and your dears

Do not let the toxic thoughts pull you down

Lift yourself up and straighten your crown

Breathe deeply and overcome this mighty fall

Times might be hard, but you will stand tall.

Overcome Procrastination

You must start now. You cannot wait until tomorrow

for things to get better.

Do not let any situation put off any dreams you are holding today.

Start with tiny steps if needed but keep moving.

Stagnancy is not going to lead you to success.

Your life is happening now, tomorrow is never guaranteed.

Overspill Positivity today

Let gratitude fill and overflow the brims of your heart today.

I am so thankful to be alive to appreciate today.

Realise how perfectly we are positioned on this planet earth in the entire solar system, for life to be able to sustain.

The fine balance of sunlight, air, water is so perfect and so is everything in our human body.

I am filled with enormous happiness to be a part of this miraculous ecosystem and this amazing harmony.

Affirmations for Today

You have never lived this day before

and you will never live this day again.

Step confidently in the direction of your dreams.

Look in the mirror and say:

I love who I have been

I have respect for who I am

I accept who I am going to be

I am going to succeed

I am bound to be happy.

Power of Prayer

The vibrations of the mind at time of praying are highest and

connected to this universal energy.

No matter where we are or what we believe, we can all use this

wonderful tool to feel the amazing power of prayer.

When my arms cannot reach people

who are close to my heart,

I always hug them with my prayers.

Winners Never Quit

I wake up with energy and the affirmation to succeed today.

Success is like the sun's golden reflection on the sand,

which no matter how many times may be covered by the waves,

still persistently shines through like a golden quartz.

When we pursue our dreams with passion and determination,

success is bound to alight upon you.

I choose to succeed and win today.

Find the Gaps to Shine Through

Each sunrise teaches us a new way to rise above all challenges

we all face every day!

It cannot continue to be cloudy always;

sunrays will find a crack to break through.

We should strive to find those gaps to fill with hope and happiness,

Become that opportunity to rise and shine.

Blissful Orange Kiss

The world is yet asleep in their complex dreams

Slowly she whispers to the waves with a gleam

Our secrets are plenty like grains of sand

Someone is making me move by pulling my hand

Let's join the dance of clouds and have some fun

Waiting eagerly for the orange kiss of the sun.

Magic in the Footsteps

It is humbling to be walking on the sand and leaving footprints,

just to be washed away by the next tide to wipe them off like a

clean slate. The realisation of how tiny we are in God's big plan.

I love the footprints on the sand

It connects me to his plan so grand

He is there beside me at this time of test

I know I am safe, and He will give me the best.

Bounce Back

When you face a minor setback in life,
bounce to make a major comeback.

It does not matter how many times you fall,

what matters is how quickly and high you bounce back.

Aspire to Inspire

Aspire to be that tiny ray of sun to bring brightness in someone's day.

A little sunshine is what someone might need today.

Believe in Goodness

The spectacular sunrise makes everything look so beautiful
under its gloss.

Happiness comes from believing in goodness.

You should be happy not because everything is good around you, but
because you are able to see the good side of everything.

Use Failures for Success

I am watching today how the waves hit the sand and how swiftly the

sand absorbs the salty water to shine back again under the sunrays.

Challenging times teach us the most and are essential

to the path of success.

May we learn to absorb, love and respect and always accept ourselves.

Liquid Gold, plenty for all

Oh heart! Breathe and behold

Let me soak in the nature's gold

Crowning blue skies with a rise so glorious

Early hours of dawn are so angelic and pious.

My Inner Radiance

What is the attraction, what is the charm?

Where is the magnet that pulls my arm?

What makes me pace so slow yet so fast?

When will this mystery unfold its cast?

Here I yearn to be one with my true glance

That which reflects through my inner radiance.

Dreams and Sandcastles

My dreams are on hold,

Ambition's on a last stand,

Falling captive to time and tide.

Like castles made of sand

Breaking but not losing pride.

Nurture Yourself

Our foremost responsibility in life is toward ourselves.

Your zest and enthusiasm towards life is your superpower.

Be selective of what you feed into your thoughts.

For in the end, only three things matter:

How much you have loved,

How graciously you lived

and how gracefully you let go of things not meant for you.

Gratitude for the Uncertainty too

Nomadic clouds are showing me the way.

Be strong, something will work out one day.

We can only get through these times by going through

and growing through these experiences.

When the caterpillar thought that the world was finishing,

just then it evolved into a butterfly.

Why the Fears?

Today sadness, anxiety and fears are overpowering,

Winds will change and sails will be to our favouring,

Hold on, overcome your fears and all you are devouring,

Winds will change and sails will be to our favouring.

Weave the Waves

Cuddle each memory and hold it tight

like a warm blanket weaved by rays of sunlight.

Waves are creating art on sand reams

And so are the mighty clouds in the sky

Let us also weave our unique dreams

To create that magical fabric called life.

Create your Destiny

Instead of feeling sad and angry about what you cannot control,

shift your energy to what you can create.

Our decisions made today will formulate our destiny for tomorrow.

Every sunshine comes full of answers.

Power of Belief to Achieve

I am looking at scattered sunrays peeping through grey thick clouds

as if indicating to me the enormous power of belief.

There is never a challenge too big for a solution not to be found.

Once I clasp strongly to my belief then I will certainly achieve.

I choose Positivity today

Just as I choose my dress from my wardrobe today, similarly I will also make a conscious choice of my thoughts from my mind's cabinet.

I shall choose to stay positive and optimistic today.

You are the Superpower

The waves are high, not an easy turf

Let us grab our board and learn to surf.

Waves might knock us down many times,

but it is only trying to show us how powerful

we can be even in our most vulnerable, rock bottom moments.

Heal and Rise Above

Nature has blessed us all with potential to self-heal and rise. You are

your own hero, the one you have been waiting for so long to help you.

But for any seed to grow into a beautiful plant it must

be de-shelled and cracked open.

Let go of any pain and imbibe the goodness around

to rise above and beyond.

My Hope Matters

The sunrise through the clouds inspires me never to lose hope.

No matter how difficult life seems at present in this pandemic.

All we need is trusting in ourselves that we will all see through

these tough times.

I choose today to face the sun and send positive vibes to all.

I have faith that they will come back to me in multiples.

I choose to wear that beautiful smile today.

Wonders of Friendship

Friendship is like the soft warmth filled by the glowing radiance

of the rising sun.

It fills your heart subtly with happiness and whispers that

everything will be alright.

Gratitude for the Shades of Grey

The struggles we face today, will shape the new reality for tomorrow.

Today it looks like someone has spilled the pot of grey in the skies.

The magnificence of greys cannot be ignored as they show the importance of sunshine.

When we cannot find the sunshine, we should aim to shine from within.

Generosity of Nature

Spectacular sunshine spreading out like a dream

Waves and sand like a radiating golden beam

Nature is generous, impartial and full of care

Be grateful for bounties and ignore not dare.

Cherish the Moments

The current situation in life has made us pause and reflect on what was missing in our life for which we have always been fighting to achieve. Both the race and pace of life were so fast that we always forgot how to live and enjoy life. We have now been given a break we deserved for a long time.

Breathe life into all the cherished moments you hold in your heart.

Prayer for Universal Peace

The serenity and calmness of this morning I pray for peace

in the whole universe.

May there be peace on the earth and may there be harmony

in all celestial objects.

Lead me from death to life, from falsehood to truth;

lead me from despair to hope, from fear to trust;

lead me from hate to love, from war to peace.

Let peace fill our heart, our world, our universe.

Appreciating the Abundance

Today is a spectacular and magical view as if, along with me, it was being witnessed by millions of angels in the sky. It fills the heart with gratitude and leaves no place for fear. Abundance is a vital aspect of enjoying the real art of living. It depicts a whole new outlook on life.

Looking for opportunities through dark moments you start appreciating beauty in smallest acts of kindness.

Let us start our day by being thankful for all that we have received and for all that is yet to come into our life.

Beautiful Relationships

Relationships are like waves harmonising in the sea.

No two waves could keep an account of sand or water they

exchange in each tide travelled to shore.

Our relations are also the blend of people in our life with

their unique existence.

Cherish the time you spend with them, the memories you create

with them in that moment.

Let us not limit ourselves by counting what we receive or what we

would offer in exchange.

Let us be limitless like waves.

Power to Forgive

Forgiveness is not weakness. It is a jewel adorned by the courageous.

You need to do it not for others but to allow yourself to move on fully

and be free of past painful memories.

'Micchami Dukkadam' is a holy day in Jainism dedicated to

forgiving everything hurtful in the past as well as asking for

forgiveness from others.

Let go of hurt, anger, and move on.

The Secret to Happiness

The secret to being happy in life is what we choose to focus on,

even when life is not perfect.

It comes from acceptance and reflection of our inner state,

whether it is in daily situations or our relationships.

Happiness is a choice.

Inhale Love, Exhale Gratitude

The power of breath is infinite.

This morning, with every incoming breath, I inhale love which is naturally surrounding me. I exhale gratitude for all the small and simple beauties of life I am blessed with.

These feelings fulfil my life with endless riches and undefinable strength gained from gratitude towards natural blessings of clean and fresh air, water, sunshine, and gift of life.

Let us count our gifts and blessings from nature.

Believe in the Gift of Today

Each morning I walk to embrace the calmness and amity of

the sunshine. The magical radiance and amber warmth casts a spell

of life given to me today as a magnificent present.

I am centring my thoughts to anchor on what can be achieved

today during this pandemic and not on thinking what may go

wrong tomorrow.

It is a precious gift to focus on just today!

"Que Sera Sera..."

The feedback from friends and posts on social media set the purpose of my daily walks as a community service. I started capturing these photos as early as 3.30 am gradually moving forward in time with the clock of the sun. The circle of friends enjoying these posts grew wider and many more people got connected to this aura of natural blessings shared through me.

For the first time, I genuinely felt the blessing of being so close to the sea and the amazing opportunity to witness the sunrise at the easternmost region in the UK. It was an uplifting experience to connect with the community by sharing the energy of the sunrise and rays of hope through these photos. Many friends came to our village to witness the sunrise and start the day with a bliss. It was like one candle lighting up other candles, forming a circle of hope and magnifying the positive energy. This appreciation has encouraged me to compile and collate some of those moments in the form of a photobook that you are holding in your hands!

Research has proven the association of sunlight with good health and healing. We find texts about how people in Ancient Egypt worshipped the Sun God as 'Ra'. In Hindu philosophy as well, there is a huge archetypal, religious and cultural significance associated with the Sun God. Prayers and Sun Salutation are associated with the belief of the sun as a giver and bestower of energy, wisdom and new forms of life. I remember a childhood memory of wrapping up my baby tooth and offering it to the sun in the hope of a pearly permanent one. Yes, the sun played the part as our tooth fairy at the time!

One of the powerful prayers called 'Aditya Hrdyam' is worshipping sun to become free from the darkness of sorrow, suffering, sin, poverty and incurable diseases. Daily meditative walks gave me the strength to recover the test of time and move to support other friends in whatever capacity.

I can now count millions of things to be grateful for in my life. My first and foremost thanks to my parents for helping me become the person I am today. My humble respect to all my teachers and mentors through my life helping me grow in dimensions of intellect and spirit. Words fall short to thank my three beautiful children Aarushi, Akshaya and Aaditya: true blessings of my life, who have stood by me in all hours to get me through these difficult times. My husband Dev has been very supportive like a rock to help me complete this book despite all odds. Supportive neighbours and community of friends are a blessing of my life. Finally, huge gratitude for Aneeta Prem, Steven Pyke, Andrea Ellis-Frost, Darren French who have been instrumental in finalising and shaping these moments into a marvellous memoir. The profits raised from this photobook are totally being distributed to the four charities close to our hearts.

I dedicate this photobook to all families who have mourned over their loved ones and friends in these difficult times to whom they were not able to say their final goodbye in person. Let us try to give radiance to their memory and be grateful for their presence in our lives. We can carry forward their best qualities and pass them down to future generations so their legacy lives on!

Let the sunshine brighten everyone's life.

Preface

Whilst leaving India in the middle of February 2020, I vividly recall assuring my mum that I'll visit again in a few weeks to spend time with her. Not knowing that the prevalence of the virus would make countries seal their borders with a complete lockdown.
By March, Covid-19 was declared as a pandemic – a global epidemiological crisis – by the World Health Organisation. It not only affected the economical and physical aspects of living but also had a huge emotional and psychological impact on people, worldwide.

We have all been living in an era of communal grief where many people are coming to terms with their individual losses daily, including illness and death due to the coronavirus or loss of employment, business, and similar life situations. During these lockdown moments, I too had the personal loss of losing my dear mother in India and not getting the chance to say a final goodbye.

My worst nightmare in this time of travel restrictions came true. I neither got to say goodbye to my mum nor embrace her for a final hug. The overwhelming emotion of not being able to say goodbye left me scarred and in a state of utter despair. I felt as if my right as a daughter had been taken away. It provoked all types of emotion including anxiety, stress, anger, frustration and sadness.

The social isolation measures have had a profound impact on the psychological and mental wellbeing of individuals across society. The only refuge I took at this time of despair was in the early morning walks to the beach near our home, in the coastal village of Hopton-on-Sea (Norfolk). The solace in the early hours of the morning came from witnessing the transformation from darkness to beautiful displays of light and brightness in a matter of seconds.

The palette of colours from the emerging sun in the sky, along with the beautiful sound of the ocean waves, was phenomenal and unique every morning. It felt as if nature wanted to fill the anxiety and hollowness with an abundance of energy and positivity. Witnessing the liquid gold spread across the sky, waves and sand was empowering me to move on with life radiantly. Even the days with dark grey clouds transforming into various shapes reminded me about the law of impermanence. They inspired me to believe that these sad days will also change and be replaced by happiness and cheer. It was an experience to see the mighty powerful ocean graciously accepting whatever the day unfolded, whether it be filled with golden-red sunshine or a sombre silver-grey.

An association with a meditation group helped me to change my outlook to one of gratitude for what I'm blessed with today rather than complain. With the number of days in lockdown continuously being extended, I became a regular sunrise watcher. It felt like an addiction to catch the colour of nature before the sun rises. It was my way of dealing with intense emotions and my own therapy towards self-healing. I started sharing these with friends through various social media platforms. Little did I realise the impact those photos had on many others who were locked indoors in isolation facing their own challenges of Covid-19.

Awakening with Sunrise

Thoughts and Quotes by Vandana Khurana

Limited Edition Photobook – in partnership with EXPERIENCE

Author details:

Vandana Khurana

Email: vandana303@aol.com

Website: www.awakeningwithsunrise.co.uk

Facebook: AwakeningwithSunrise

Twitter: @vandana303

ISBN 978 1 80 049179 3

Copyright © 2020 Vandana Khurana

This edition of Awakening with Sunrise has been reprinted in partnership with EXPERIENCE and forms part of a meditative experiential journey. To find out more visit:

www.tourismexperience.org

EUROPEAN UNION

Interreg

France (Channel / Manche) England

EXPERIENCE
European Regional Development Fund